KU-104-298

ACC. No:  06002155

HOW TO READ AND INTERPRET

# RUNES

HOW TO READ AND INTERPRET

# RUNES

Using runes for divination, protection, healing and understanding

ANDY BAGGOTT

LORENZ BOOKS

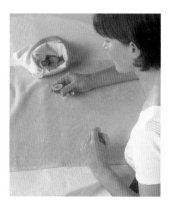

This edition is published by Lorenz Books,
an imprint of Anness Publishing Ltd,
Blaby Road, Wigston, Leicestershire LE18 4SE;
info@anness.com

www.lorenzbooks.com; www.annesspublishing.com

If you like the images in this book and would like to
investigate using them for publishing, promotions or advertising,
please visit our website www.practicalpictures.com
for more information.

Publisher: Joanna Lorenz
Project Editor: Sarah Duffin
Designer: Lesley Betts
Photographer: Don Last
Illustrator: Nadine Wickenden

© Anness Publishing Ltd 2012

All rights reserved. No part of this publication
may be reproduced, stored in a retrieval system,
or transmitted in any way or by any means, electronic,
mechanical, photocopying, recording or otherwise,
without the prior written permission
of the copyright holder.

A CIP catalogue record for this book is available
from the British Library.

PUBLISHER'S NOTE
The reader should not regard the recommendations, ideas and
techniques expressed and described in this book as substitutes for
the advice of a qualified medical practitioner or other qualified
professional. Any use to which the recommendations, ideas and
techniques are put is at the reader's sole discretion and risk.

# CONTENTS

# INTRODUCTION

PART OF THE PURPOSE OF LIFE is to learn lessons and gain knowledge and wisdom. Since the dawn of time, humankind has found signs and symbols fascinating and powerful. The power of the runes comes in what they have to teach us. The runes present lessons to us and, if used wisely, can facilitate the learning of those lessons quickly and efficiently.

The runes do not provide the answers to all of life's problems. Neither do they imbue their user with magical powers. They do, however, present signposts to direct us on our journey through life. The purpose of this book is to demonstrate how to read those signposts, and to give guidance on lesson learning.

The runes represent certain images, and it is by working with these images that the guidance and teaching of the runes becomes accessible to all. The lore of rune-casting was once the domain of a chosen few, in a time when only a minority sought spiritual enlightenment. Today, many people are seeking answers to questions, and it is right that these "seekers of wisdom" should have access to clear instruction regarding this ancient oracle.

This book is designed to be a highly practical work which gives the reader full instructions on working with runes. There is guidance about the making of your own rune set and how to use it. The casting of runes, in this book, goes from simple one- or three-rune draws to more complex spreads using up to nine runes.

The imagery and meaning of each individual rune is featured at the back of the book in an easy reference guide that is designed to form a base from which individuals can develop the ideas presented and study further. The photographs will give the reader more of a sense of the runes and offer some ideas about using and working with runes that go beyond simple divination.

As a daily practising shaman of the Celtic tradition, runes have formed part of my spiritual tradition. They have taught me many lessons and given me access to greater wisdom. The way of the runes is subtle but powerful and can have a profound effect on many levels. This book will show how runes are used not only for divination, but for protection, healing, empowerment and learning. For many years, I have listened to people say that they find the runes difficult to understand, that the books about runes are sometimes confusing or too in-depth. It was for this reason that this book was written – to make runic wisdom accessible to all through simple instruction and clear illustration.

The mystery of the runes is not a mystery at all, it is simply a path towards greater learning that anyone can tread.

Andy Baggott

# THE HISTORY OF THE RUNES

DETAIL OF RUNES ON A
SCANDINAVIAN RUNE STONE.

THE ORIGIN of the runes is uncertain, although archeological finds with runic inscriptions have been dated from 3AD onwards. The runes were a sacred writing system used throughout the Germanic tribes of northern Europe, especially among those of Britain, Scandinavia and Iceland. In some places this writing system was used until the 17th century, appearing on memorial stones, weapons, tools and buildings. The angular nature of the runes implies a pre-Christian origin, although scholars are divided on this issue.

This angular script points to the fact that they were not intended for writing but for carving. This is confirmed by the numerous stone memorials bearing runes and by the scarcity of written manuscripts. Significantly, the word "rune" comes from the root *runa* – "a whisper" or "a secret" – which points to a magical use.

There are many different varieties of runic writing, ranging from the Early or Elder Germanic script of 24 letters, the Anglo-Saxon script with an original 28 letters rising to 33, to varieties of Nordic, Danish and Swedish runic alphabets varying from 15 to 16 letters. There are in excess of 4,000 runic inscriptions and several runic manuscripts still in existence today, with a vast majority of them – some 2,500 – originating from Sweden. The other runic inscriptions are mainly to be found in Norway, Denmark, Britain and Iceland, although some have also been discovered on various islands off the coasts of Britain and Scandinavia, as well as in France, Germany and the former Soviet Union.

It is now known that there existed shaman-like medicine men and women throughout northern Europe, with a complex and deep spiritual tradition of which the runes were an intrinsic part. Initiatory practices such as repetitive chants (called *Galdr*) and ritual body positions (called *Stadha*) were associated with the runes, and a runemaster was held in the highest esteem.

RUNIC INSCRIPTION ON
THE JELLING STONE.

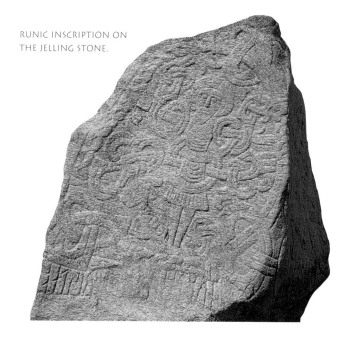

## RUNES PAST AND PRESENT

In the past, there were two main types of people who worked with the runes: runecutters, who had a limited knowledge of the runes and their general protective qualities, and runemasters (male and female), who had undergone many initiatory experiences to discover the deeper secrets of rune lore. These runemasters knew not only how to divine successfully with runes, but also how to use runes to their advantage in magical and healing work.

Since the beginning of the 20th century, runes have been growing in popularity. Many books about runes are now available, and there are even schools teaching runic divination and the finer arts of rune lore. The fact that runes have lasted the whole millennium is an indication that they are here to stay and that their potential power has been undiminished by the years.

## THE RUNIC ALPHABET

The most widely used alphabet is the Early Germanic or Elder Futhark, which is used in this book. The word "futhark" refers to the first six runic letters, whose English equivalents are f, u, th, a, r and k. In the same way, our word "alphabet" refers to the first two letters of the Greek alphabet, alpha (or a) and beta (or b). Each runestone depicts one letter from the runic alphabet.

The letters of the elder futhark are divided into three groups of eight letters called aetts, as follows:

F U Th A R K G W

H N I J Y P Z S

T B E M L Ng D O

Here is the English alphabet with its equivalent runes (there are no equivalent runes for the letters c, q and v):

A B C D E F G H I J K L M N O P Q R S T U V W X Y Z

RUNE STONE WITH THE OLDEST EVER KNOWN REPRESENTATION OF THE ELDER FUTHARK IN SWEDEN.

## NORSE MYTHOLOGY

Rune lore is closely linked to the long spiritual history of the Scandinavians and their gods and goddesses. Many writings exist (called sagas) that tell of the works of the Norse gods and goddesses. In Norse mythology, the chief god is Odin, the all-father, the discoverer of the runes and the first runemaster. He was married to Frigg and together they had two sons, Balder (the beautiful god) and Thor (the thunder god). Odin also had a blood brother called Loki who played the part of the trickster throughout the sagas.

ODIN.

THOR.

LOKI (RIGHT) WITH HODR.

FREY.

There is also Njord, the god of the sea, whose children are Frey (the fertility god) and Freya (the goddess of war, love and magic). Many other gods and goddesses are mentioned throughout the sagas, including Heimdal (the shining god), Bragi (the god of poetry), Idun (the goddess of healing and the wife of Bragi) and Tyr (the warrior god).

With the spread of Christianity came attempts to suppress the old religions; runes were used on memorials until the 17th century, but much of their magical use was hidden from public knowledge and has only emerged with the present-day growth of interest in all ancient traditions.

## THE LEGEND OF ODIN AND THE RUNES

In Norse mythology, the god Odin experienced a shamanic initiation during which time the runes appeared to him. Legend tells that he hung upside down for nine days and nights upon Yggdrasil, the World Tree or Tree of Life, which is said to be an ash tree. The following poem, which is an extract from a Norse Saga, recounts the tale from Odin's perspective:

*I know, that I hung*
*on the windy tree*
*all of nights nine,*
*wounded by spear*
*and given to Odin;*
*myself to myself,*
*on that tree*
*which no man knows*
*from what roots it rises.*
*They dealt me no bread*
*nor drinking horn;*
*I looked down,*
*I took up the runes,*
*I took them screaming,*
*I fell back from there.*

The practice of subjecting one's body to extremes of deprivation and suffering is well known to promote visions, and it is probable that the runes originally grew from a shamanic vision such as the one described above.

ODIN IS OFTEN LINKED TO THE "HANGED MAN" OF THE TAROT CARDS.

# CREATING YOUR OWN RUNE SET

IF YOU WANT TO GET TO KNOW the runes, it is vital that you create your own rune set, rather than buying one ready made. This takes time and energy, but it gives you a much more intimate relationship with the runes. The two materials from which runes are commonly made are wood and stone, although other materials, such as crystals, glass beads or clay, can also be used.

1 Collect 24 stones for your rune set. Using a fine paintbrush and natural-coloured acrylic paint, paint the runic inscriptions on each stone.

2 When the paint is dry, apply a coat of varnish over the stones to protect the paint.

## USING STONES

Wherever you go in the world, there are always stones to be found. Some of the best stones for rune making can be found on beaches and in stream beds. The Nordic and Celtic people believed that every stone has a spirit within it which needs to be honoured if it is to work well for you, so it is important to leave a small offering at any place where you take something from creation. The traditional offering is sea salt as it is said to be formed by the fusion of the four primal elements – Earth, Air, Fire and Water. Alternative offerings include tobacco (which is sacred to the Native Americans), corn (which is sacred throughout the Old World) and coloured ribbon.

THE COMPLETED STONE RUNE SET.

## USING WOOD

The three favoured types of wood for rune making are ash (the World Tree), yew (the rune Eoh) and birch (the rune Beorc), as they have direct connections to the runes. However, the following trees can also be used for fashioning magical tools and are given here with their principal symbology:

ROWAN - A PROTECTIVE TREE
WILLOW - A TREE CONNECTED STRONGLY WITH THE MOON
OAK - SYMBOLIC OF STRENGTH
HAZEL - MUCH FAVOURED BY DIVINERS THROUGHOUT THE AGES
APPLE - LINKED TO LOVE
BLACKTHORN - MASCULINE SYMBOL OF SPIRITUAL AUTHORITY
HAWTHORN - BLACKTHORN'S PROTECTIVE SISTER TREE

3 Using a handsaw, carefully cut the branch into slices for the 24 runes, about 2–5cm (³/₄–2in) across.

4 Using a poker or a pyrography or soldering iron, carefully burn the runic inscriptions into each rune.

1 Before cutting a branch, ask permission from the tree by placing your hands on its trunk and saying a short prayer.

2 Sprinkle a small offering of sea salt at the base of the tree to honour it before cutting off a small branch.

5 Dip a soft cloth in natural beeswax and rub this over each rune to protect the wood.

THE COMPLETED WOODEN RUNE SET.

## CLEANSING YOUR RUNES

Once you have made your runes, it is important to cleanse them spiritually. This can be done in a variety of ways: they can be laid out under a full moon for a night, or you can waft smoking herbs over them (called "smudging"), or, more simply, they can be cleansed using naturally flowing water from a well, spring or stream. Do not use tap water as it is full of man-made chemicals that are bad for everything, including humans!

## EMPOWERING YOUR RUNES

Once you have cleansed your runes, you need to empower them. Again, this can be done in a variety of ways. Some runemasters lay their runes out in the midday summer sun, while others bury them in the earth for nine days. Here, the power of the four elements has been used to empower the runes.

1 Sprinkle sea salt by a stream to honour it before cleansing your runes. Say a prayer asking for permission.

2 Place your runes in a bag and dip it in the stream, for a short while or overnight – let your intuition guide you.

1 Place the runes on a cloth and sprinkle with sea salt to empower the runes with Earth.

2 Pass each rune through incense smoke while asking the element of Air to empower the runes.

3 Then pass each rune individually through a candle flame to empower the runes with Fire.

4 For the final stage, sprinkle spring water over the runes to empower them with Water.

## CARE OF YOUR RUNES

Runes can be powerful and helpful allies provided that you treat them with the care and respect they deserve. Remember that having cleansed and empowered your runes, they are imbued with your own unique energy and they should never be lent to anyone for them to use. This does not mean that other people cannot touch your runes; on the contrary, it is sometimes essential for someone else to touch them, especially if you are giving them a reading and you need them to focus on the runes. But no one else should work with your runes for themselves.

As you work with your runes, especially if you do a lot of readings for others, you will need to cleanse them regularly. You may also want to perform an annual re-empowering ceremony. After a while, as you get to know your runes better, they will let you know when they need cleansing: they will start to feel uncomfortable to hold. If this happens, simply re-cleanse them. If your runes have been locked away for any period of time, you will need to re-energize them with the energies of the sun and moon by laying them outside for 24 hours.

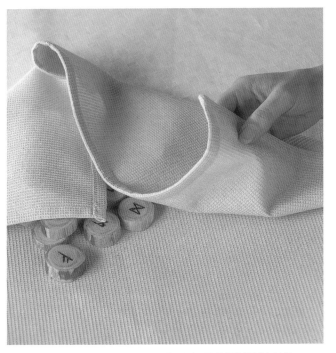

FABRIC CAN BE USED BOTH TO WRAP THE RUNES IN AND TO LAY DOWN AS A CASTING CLOTH.

A RUNE BAG IS ESSENTIAL FOR STORING THE RUNES.

# LEARNING FROM THE RUNES

EVERYTHING IN THE UNIVERSE is vibrating; nothing is still. Some things vibrate harmoniously while others vibrate discordantly. Anything that is balanced and "healthy" has a harmonious vibration. Anything that is unbalanced and "unhealthy" has a discordant vibration. All natural things, such as plants, animals and crystals, when not tampered with by man, have harmonious vibrations.

Ultimately human beings are seeking balance and harmony. The runes present symbols whose vibrations help us to learn lessons that will enable us to become more balanced. They are like a series of lost chords that we need to find. Each rune has a corresponding tree, colour, herb and crystal. These are naturally occurring things whose vibrations can help us to understand better the lessons of the runes. They each hold some of the notes of the lost chords.

To begin to learn from the runes, one needs to "tune-in" to their vibrations. Working with the corresponding tree, colour, herb and crystal, one can set up a vibrational field that allows the subconscious mind to learn the vibration and teach its lesson to the conscious mind. Instead of using the conscious mind to try to find the lesson of each rune, you can allow the lesson to find you.

LEARN THE LESSONS OF BALANCE
AND HARMONY FROM NATURE.

The ancient Celts and Vikings, in common with all people who live in balance and harmony with creation, believed that everything in nature has a "spirit", an energy that can be communicated with and learnt from. This not only included trees, herbs and crystals, but also stones and even runes. Through techniques of mind control and meditation, they were able to "tune-in" to the vibrations of these things and learn from them.

By meditating with gifts from nature, you will experience their vibrations. The first step is simply to touch, feel, hold, smell and meditate with them. The vast array of images and sensations that these offer will become easier to understand as you work with the runes.

## MEDITATING WITH YOUR PERSONAL RUNE

Hold the bag containing all your runes and empty your mind of all mundane thoughts. Ask the runes to show you your personal power rune which will be your guide. Pick out a single rune from the bag and hold it in your hand and meditate for a while, noting any images and thoughts that enter your mind.

Each rune has a corresponding tree, colour, herb and crystal. These are keys that unlock the lessons of the rune. You may wish to wear the colour and meditate beside the tree while holding the herb and crystal. If you have no access to these, picture them clearly in your mind before you begin to meditate. Ask to be shown some of the lessons that your power rune has to teach you. These will often appear as images that enter your mind and

MEDITATING WITH ANGELICA FLOWERS WILL HELP YOU TO UNLOCK THE MEANING OF THE CORRESPONDING POWER RUNE.

MEDITATING WITH YEW FRONDS AND A BLUE RIBBON WILL HELP YOU TO ACCESS THE LESSONS OF THE EOH RUNE.

should be noted down in a book. Consider what they may mean or the messages they hold for you. Do not worry if you cannot interpret them all as some of the lessons may only reveal themselves with time and patience. You cannot force understanding.

When you have worked with your power rune for a while, you may wish to research the corresponding tree, colour, herb and crystal – each has healing properties that may give you clues as to the areas of your life that need healing and the lessons you need to learn. For example, the oak teaches strength but warns against inflexibility, as it is easily felled in a storm.

The willow, on the other hand, teaches this flexibility as it bends in the wind. Even if a piece of it is broken off, that piece will root and grow into a new tree; so it also teaches the power of regeneration.

# CONSULTING THE RUNES

WHENEVER YOU HAVE A problem for which you can find no solution, a question for which you can find no answer or a decision you cannot make, you can consult the runes. They will not tell you precisely what to do or how to act. But what they will do is comment on a situation, giving you a new perspective from which to view things. This in turn will give you greater objectivity, which will then help you in your decision making. The wisdom of the runes is more subtle than a simple "yes" or "no" answer. If this is what you want, you will have to flip a coin!

Divination works in the following way. If you have a problem or an issue for which you need guidance, you can focus your thoughts on that problem while holding your rune bag. This will send a vibration into the runes. The rune or runes that can provide guidance about the issue will resonate and you will unconsciously be attracted to pick out these runes. The more focused your thinking is, the clearer the answer will be. When focusing on the problem, ask the runes to comment on the issue rather than asking them a "yes" or "no" question.

If, for instance, you are undecided whether to move into a new house or not, rather than asking the runes, "Should I move into a new house?", you should say, "I would like the runes to comment on the issue of whether I should move into a new house or not". Likewise, if you are

CONSULT THE RUNES WHEN YOU NEED GUIDANCE. THE MORE FOCUSED YOUR THINKING IS, THE CLEARER THE ANSWERS WILL BE FROM THE RUNES.

asking about a possible partner in love, you should ask the runes to comment on your relationship rather than just asking, "Is this the right person for me?"

Once you have done this, you can draw runes in one of two ways. You can pick individual runes out of the bag and lay them on your casting cloth in front of you. Alternatively, you can place all the runes in front of you, face down upon the casting cloth, and pass your hand over them, picking the rune that your hand feels most attracted to. This attraction may manifest itself as a warm, tingling sensation in your hand when it passes over the right rune for you. Once you have chosen a rune, turn it over from left to right and place it in front of you.

When drawing a rune, it is important that you have a clear intent about the way in which you want the rune to comment. If you wish it to give you a general perspective upon an issue, you only need to draw a single rune. However, you may wish the runes to comment on a number of points relating to an issue: for example, what has led up to the issue occurring in your life (the past), how you should approach it now (the present) and what the possible outcome could be (the future). In this case, you need to draw three runes, holding one of these aspects clearly in your mind before you draw each rune. In this way you can achieve quite specific guidance which will be of great help on your journey through life.

The power of interpretation is available to everyone and it improves with practice. There are specific ways to improve your readings and interpretations which will come with patience and a little discipline. Each time you perform a reading with the runes, make a note of the issue on which you are asking the runes to comment, which runes you draw, and what you think they mean. About a month later, go back and look again at the comments you wrote, noting down any new insights that you have gained between the time of the readings and the present. This will help you to evaluate which parts of your original interpretation were accurate, and which were not. In this way, you will be able to improve your skills and understand more clearly what the runes have to say to you, the way that they say it and how you can learn from them.

## METHOD 2

1 Concentrate on what you want to ask before you draw a rune. Then pick individual runes out of the bag.

2 Once you have picked a rune, turn it over from left to right and place it on your casting cloth in front of you.

## METHOD 1

1 Place all the runes face down upon the casting cloth. Pass your hand over them to find which runes you are attracted to.

2 When your hand passes over the right rune, it may become warm and tingling. Turn the rune over from left to right and place it in front of you.

# INTERPRETING THE RUNES

To become adept at interpreting the runes it is important to train your intuition, for this is the connection to your higher self, the part of your being that knows everything. It knows your purpose in life and how that purpose can best be achieved. It also knows the purpose of everyone you meet and so knows how best you can guide those people who seek your help. Training the intuition allows you access to that knowledge and the runes can act as catalysts in this process.

## TRAINING THE INTUITION THROUGH MEDITATION

Meditation is a most efficient way of training the intuition because to hear the guiding voice of your higher self, you must have a mind that is in a receptive state to receive those messages. Whenever you pick out a rune to interpret, it is important to meditate with that rune to access your intuition. The following exercise shows you how to do this.

Settle yourself in a place where you feel relaxed; this can be outside or in a dimly lit room. Make sure that you will not be disturbed by telephones or people. You may wish to light a candle to help you to focus your mind. Sit in a comfortable position, hold your rune bag in your hands and close your eyes. Take a few deep breaths and imagine every muscle in your body relaxing. Now you need to empty your mind of all thoughts and to quieten its chatter. Try to focus on your breathing or picture yourself beside a beautiful lake. Every time a thought pops into your mind, allow it to leave and refocus upon your breathing or upon the image of the lake.

When you feel ready, without opening your eyes, pick out a single rune and hold it in your hand. Try to tune into its vibration while asking the rune to speak to you. Allow your mind to become open so that different images and thoughts can enter it. Do this for as long as it feels comfortable. When you feel ready, thank the rune for speaking to you and then open your eyes and look at the rune. Make a note of all the images and messages that came into your mind. Now look up the meaning of the rune and see how this relates to

MEDITATING WITH A RUNE ENABLES YOU TO ACCESS YOUR INTUITION.

what you felt during your meditation. Note the differences and similarities between the images that you felt during your meditation and the images and lessons given in the book. Now meditate again, asking the rune to show you how all these different images fit together, then note down all your thoughts and impressions.

As you work more with the runes, you will be able to review exercises such as the one above and any points that seemed unclear will become clearer as you gain more understanding. The trick is to be patient. The runes reveal different aspects of themselves only when they know you are ready to learn them.

## REVERSED MEANINGS

Some of the runes reveal a different sign when viewed upside down. These are called reverse runes. When you

THE MEANING OF THE RUNE FEOH IS WEALTH AND RICHNESS.

THE REVERSED MEANING OF THE RUNE FEOH IS DISCOVERING RICHNESS.

turn over a rune and it is upside down it has a separate meaning to when it is the correct way up. Many people used to regard reversed meanings as negative. For instance, the first rune – Feoh – has an image of wealth and richness, so many people regarded Feoh reversed as having an image of poverty. This is incorrect.

Each rune has its own lessons to teach. An upright rune has an image that teaches us something. If the rune is reversed, it means that the lessons of the upright are what we are lacking and therefore what we need to strive for. Therefore, the image of Feoh reversed does not mean "poverty", but "discovering richness". The difference is subtle but very important. The reversed meanings do not show problems, but solutions. One should always look at every rune in terms of what it has to teach, rather than looking at the negative aspects of the rune.

# THE SINGLE RUNE

ONE CAN DRAW a single rune for a variety of reasons: to act as a guiding rune for the day; to act as a guide before beginning a project; or to gain further insight into a problem. The single rune gives you an overview of an issue or of what lies ahead, and is often all the guidance one needs. It is simple, quick and effective.

Before drawing a single rune, hold your rune bag while focusing on the issue upon which you wish the runes to comment. You may wish to say one of the following:
1. "I wish the runes to comment upon the day ahead."
2. "I wish the runes to comment upon (name a future endeavour)."
3. "I wish the runes to comment upon (name an issue or problem)."

Then pick a single rune by one of the two methods shown earlier. Meditate while holding that rune, then look up its meaning.

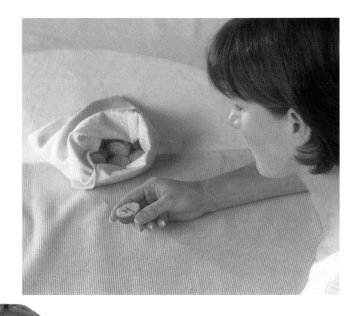

THE RUNE HAGALL
MEANS A CHALLENGE.

### SAMPLE READING NO 1.

Susan had been looking for a partner for some time. She had had a series of short relationships with men with whom she discovered she was incompatible. She was beginning to feel that she was not meant to be happy in love and so asked the runes to comment upon her love life. She drew Hagall.

**Meaning:** The rune told Susan of the need to hold on to her dream and that instead of looking for the perfect man, she should allow that perfect man to find her. It also said that she should concentrate on her lessons, trusting that every challenge that she faced was a stepping stone to the realization of that dream. She understood this clearly and changed her attitude to life by resolving to embrace every challenge and concentrate upon learning her lessons as they came to her. Shortly afterwards she met her perfect man and they have just bought their first home together.

## SAMPLE READING NO 2.

John was looking for a new house. He had found a property that he liked but the process of buying the house was presenting some problems. He wanted to know if this was the right house for him, because he did not want to waste energy on the property if the purchase was going to fall through. He asked the runes to comment upon the issue of him buying the property, and picked out Geofu. **Meaning:** A gift was coming to John (the house) but he would need to give something of himself (energy) before it would become part of his life. This giving would teach him valuable lessons that would help him along his path. So John persevered and the purchase went through without further problems.

## SAMPLE READING NO 3.

Tony had just been made redundant from a job that he did not like. While relieved to be free from it, he was fearful for his future and concerned about finding new employment. He asked the runes to comment about this, and drew Rad. **Meaning:** Tony learned that he had just come to the end of a cycle in his life. He needed to live in the present and learn its lessons while trusting that the future would only provide him with valuable opportunities to learn more. After several failed interviews for jobs in the same field as his last one (which he had not enjoyed), he realized that the lesson was that he needed a different type of job. He decided to look for a job in the open countryside and now thoroughly enjoys his work.

# THE THREE-RUNE SPREAD

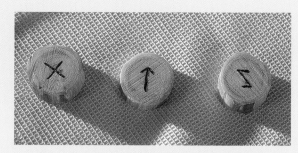

THE THREE-RUNE SPREAD OF GEOFU, TYR AND EOH.

T HE THREE-RUNE SPREAD is particularly useful in giving an overall picture of an issue. It places the issue in its context by showing the events that have led up to it, the issue itself and, finally, the most likely future outcome. The three-rune spread is like a signpost at a crossroads showing where you are, where you have been and where you can potentially go if you learn the lessons you need to learn.

For the three-rune spread, the runes are laid out as follows:

1. Past          2. Present          3. Future

Once you have thought for some time on an issue and have it clearly fixed in your mind, draw your first rune. While focusing on the rune you draw, think of the events that have led up to the issue or how you have attracted the issue into your life. Now draw your second rune, and while focusing on the rune consider the present moment regarding the issue. Finally, draw your third rune, focusing on your wish to be shown where the issue is taking you or what the possible future outcome will be. It is important to focus on what each rune represents when drawing it. The stronger your focus and intent, the clearer your answers will be.

## SAMPLE READING NO 1.

Anne had been suffering from ill-health for over six months. She had consulted both medical doctors and alternative health practitioners but to no avail. She did not understand why her illness kept returning, whatever she did to fight it. She drew the following three runes: Geofu, Tyr and Eoh.

**Meaning:** The rune Geofu showed Anne that her illness was a gift which she was trying to reject instead of accepting. The gift was the lessons the illness had to teach her. Tyr showed Anne that if she remained true to herself and her beliefs, she would gain victory over her illness. Eoh showed Anne that major change was coming and that by embracing the future while letting go of the past, she would enter a new phase of her life. Anne realized that the cure to her illness lay within her. She dealt with several unresolved issues from the past and was quickly restored to health.

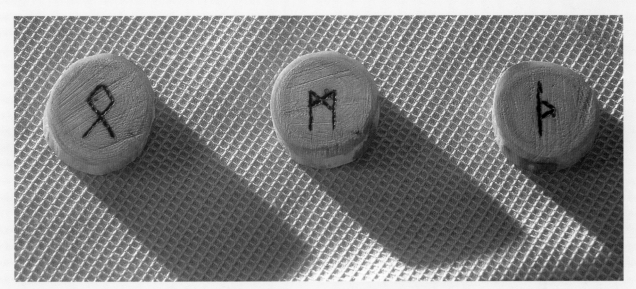

THE THREE-RUNE SPREAD OF OTHEL, MANN AND THORN.

## SAMPLE READING NO 2.

James had spent the previous year abroad, living a spiritual life with an indigenous tribe. Having returned to his home in England, he felt as though he had lost everything that he had learned. He was confused and felt disconnected from his family and friends. He drew Othel, Mann and Thorn.

**Meaning:** Othel spoke to James of the time of focus and freedom which he had enjoyed while away from western civilization. It also indicated that perhaps he was trying to hold on to this feeling which was clouding his dream of being truly free.

Mann showed James that he had lost nothing; everything he thought he had lost was actually waiting for him to claim. This rune also showed him that the feelings he was having needed to be embraced so that he could learn from them. Thorn showed James that he need not fear anything. He needed to be humble rather than arrogant, and he would then be able to recapture all that he felt he had lost. From this, James learnt to integrate all the wisdom he had gained from his time away into his life and to share it humbly with others.

# ADVANCED DIVINATION

THE RUNES CAN BE USED to give deeper insights to help you on your spiritual path. The following spreads are designed to help you understand and learn from the lessons that life is giving you. Some of the later spreads use many runes; you can either replace the runes between draws, having noted each one down, so that you always have 24 runes to draw from, or you may feel you wish to draw the runes as before, without replacing them. It is up to your intuition. There is no right or wrong way to do this.

## THE FOUR-ELEMENT SPREAD

The Nordic tradition views the four elements of Earth, Water, Fire and Air as the building blocks of the universe, and they assign a different direction and quality to each element. The north is the place of Earth, the west of Water, the south of Fire, and the east of Air. By compiling a spread where the runes are positioned at each point of the compass, each rune is imbued with the qualities of its corresponding element.

STREAM REPRESENTS WATER, WHICH IS SYMBOLIC OF EMOTIONAL BALANCE AND GOING WITH THE FLOW.

SEA SALT REPRESENTS EARTH, WHICH IS SYMBOLIC OF ALL PHYSICAL LESSONS IN OUR LIVES.

CANDLE FLAME REPRESENTS FIRE, WHICH IS SYMBOLIC OF HOW WE EXPRESS OUR LIVES AND SPIRITUAL PATH.

SMOKE REPRESENTS AIR, WHICH IS SYMBOLIC OF TURNING KNOWLEDGE INTO WISDOM.

1. Earth – This is situated in the north of the spread. It has a downward, grounding pull and represents all your physical lessons.

2. Water – Positioned to the west, this is an upward and buoyant sign and represents all your emotional lessons.

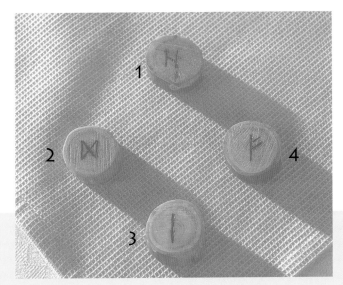

3. Fire – At the south of the spread, fire represents your spiritual lessons and is closely linked to your unfolding destiny.

4. Air – Positioned to the east, air can draw in knowledge and therefore represents the place where you should seek wisdom for the future.

THE FOUR-ELEMENT SPREAD OF HAGALL, DAEG, IS AND FEOH REVERSED.

## SAMPLE READING

Jenny had just lost her mother. Although it did not come as a shock, she was still having problems dealing with it. She asked the runes for help and guidance and drew the following: Hagall, Daeg, Is and Feoh reversed.

**Meaning:** Hagall spoke of a challenge on the physical level. Jenny understood this to mean the physical challenge involved in organizing her mother's funeral, and that although times were hard at present, they would not last forever. Daeg spoke of a light and Jenny realized she had been emotionally in a very dark place. It also reminded her that her mother was now in the light

and this gave her great comfort. Is showed Jenny the need for patience and the importance of allowing the grieving process to unfold, of using this time to look back over her life with her mother and to recognize all the lessons she had learnt from this.

Feoh showed Jenny that she needed to acknowledge the rich gifts of love and teaching that her mother had given her. It reminded her that no one can take her memories away from her. This reading proved a source of great strength and inspiration for Jenny during this difficult time in her life.

# THE WORLD TREE SPREAD

THE WORLD TREE is one of the oldest and most universal symbols in the world. Images of a sacred tree appear among most earth-based belief systems and in such religions as Christianity and Kabbalism. In the Nordic tradition, Yggdrasil was the sacred ash tree of life and death. The roots of the tree are said to connect to the underworld, which is inhabited by many nature spirits, plant divas and elementals. By descending the tree while in a visionary state, the shaman could seek guidance and wisdom from these beings. The upper branches of the tree are said to ascend to the upper world, which is inhabited by angels, advanced souls and supernatural entities who are again sought out by the shaman on his visionary journeys. Some representations of the world tree also show the leaves and branches inhabited by discarnate souls either on their way to or from the earthly plane.

The world tree is a powerful archetypal image and a source of great wisdom and knowledge.

STONE CARVING OF YGGDRASIL, THE WORLD TREE.

For this reason, the world tree spread is designed to act as a guide to the next stage of your spiritual journey, giving knowledge about the next lesson you can learn, the next challenge that lies ahead, your guides, allies, omens and more. It is designed to speed you along your adventurous path towards new enlightenments, teaching you that everything that enters your life gives you an opportunity for learning so that you can become a better, stronger and wiser person.

The spread begins at the earth and rises up the trunk of the tree towards the heavens. It represents a phase of your spiritual journey, and this image should be clearly fixed in your mind when using the spread. Here you are using the runes as an oracle. You are not coming with a question or a problem, just an open heart, eager to learn how to make swift and sure progress on your path of learning. In this spread, the runes speak directly to you and for you. Listen to their wisdom.

SAMPLE WORLD TREE SPREAD.

The positions have the following meanings:

1. What do you need to learn?
2. What will challenge you?
3. What is your guiding rune?
4. What power will help you?
5. What comes to warn you?
6. What do you need to let go of?
7. What will be the outcome of learning this lesson?

## SAMPLE READING

1. Nied. You need to learn that the past is just a memory and the future just a dream; the present is the only place where you can have influence.

2. Tyr reversed. You are challenged to look honestly at your weaknesses and resolve to turn them into strengths.

3. Peorth. Your guiding rune tells you to remember that you always have a choice in everything.

4. Feoh. The power behind you comes from the fact that you have a spiritual richness that is to be used for the benefit of all.

5. Hagall. You are warned that challenges are entering your life and that these are not to be feared, rather embraced.

6. Elhaz. You need to let go of fear for you have the power of protection within you.

7. Jara. This will lead to a time of reaping rewards for the seeds sown in the past.

# CLARIFYING UNCLEAR ANSWERS

SOMETIMES after consulting the runes, things seem no clearer than they were before the reading, and you are left uncertain as to how to interpret them. The runes can occasionally be ambiguous, particularly if the question you are asking is not entirely

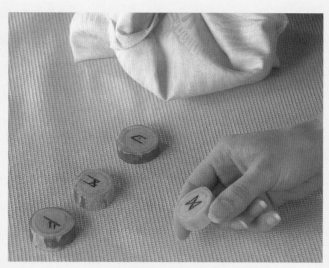

straightforward. If this is the case, it may be necessary to draw an extra rune. This is done simply by asking the runes to provide a better explanation, and then drawing a single rune which should clarify the message the runes are trying to give.

IF THE RUNES ARE AMBIGUOUS, ASK THEM TO SHOW YOU MORE CLARITY, THEN DRAW A SINGLE EXTRA RUNE.

## SAMPLE READING

David had been plagued by nightmares for some time and was seeking help in curing them. He had been considering the idea of seeking out a colour therapist, although his family would have preferred him to go to a conventional counsellor for treatment. The nightmares were becoming unbearable and David wanted to get better as quickly as possible. He asked the runes to guide him in the right direction so he could find the best way to treat his problem. He used the three-rune spread and drew the following runes: Feoh reversed (the past), Mann reversed (the present) and Ur (the future).

**Meaning:** Feoh reversed told David that the root of his problem came from emotional imbalances. Mann reversed showed him that he had to make his own choice. Ur showed that, once healed, David would have the strength to fulfill his dreams.

This was all very positive, but David was still unsure which therapy to choose and so drew a clarifying rune. The rune was Daeg, which speaks of the power of the light. He knew then that colour therapy was the correct treatment for him; this quickly freed him from his nightmares and he was able to continue upon his path.

# CREATING YOUR OWN SPREADS

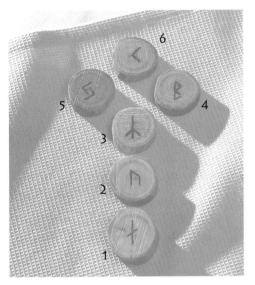

CELTIC CROSS SPREAD.

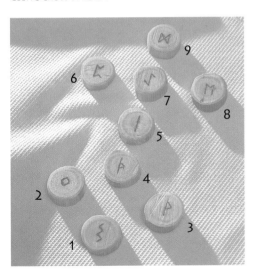

THOR'S HAMMER SPREAD.

THE SPREADS GIVEN HERE are starting points to show you the range and flexibility of the runes. You can create your own spreads and decide what you want each rune to represent. As long as you maintain a strong intent when drawing each rune, they will give you guidance about anything. Here are two more complex spreads for you to try out.

## THE CELTIC CROSS SPREAD:

1. What is the root of your lack of clarity?
2. How and where should you direct your energies?
3. What is blocking your progress?
4. What will help you overcome this blockage?
5. What are you still lacking?
6. What will be the outcome of this experience?

## THOR'S HAMMER SPREAD:

1. What mask do you show the world?
2. What fears are within you?
3. What are you seeking?
4. How should you best approach this?
5. What do you hope to become?
6. What is stopping you?
7. What is your destiny?
8. What do you need to learn to find your true self?
9. What is your true self?

THE CELTIC CROSS ENGRAVED WITH SPIRALS REPRESENTING SPIRALS OF LEARNING.

THOR'S HAMMER HARNESSES THE ENERGY OF THOR.

# RUNE MAGIC

THERE IS NOTHING MYSTICAL about magic. Magic comes from an understanding of the subtle vibrations that emanate from all things. Rune magic teaches how you can attune yourself to individual runes.

## EMPOWERING YOURSELF

As you work with the runes, they will teach you about the power of nature. By working with trees, colour, herbs and crystals, you will begin to understand more about your connection to and place in the universe. Nature teaches balance and harmony, for she is always seeking them. Whenever man upsets the natural balance of the world, nature always returns the balance if given the opportunity. Just visiting a disused quarry or railway line will show you the amazing power that nature has to reclaim and re-colonize the land.

Nature teaches by example and through vibrations, so regular communing with nature can be both enlightening and empowering. If you want to find your true connection, spend time among nature enjoying its beauty.

WEARING A RUNE FOCUSES ITS QUALITIES AND ENERGIES INTO YOUR LIFE.

MEDITATE WITH PLANTS AND TREES; THEY WILL TEACH AND GUIDE YOU IF YOU ARE PATIENT.

## WEARING RUNES

Another way to empower yourself is to wear a rune around your neck. Runes emit powerful vibrations and by wearing a rune about your neck, you subject the whole of your being to that positive vibration. This will have a protective effect and will also attract the qualities of that rune into your life.

## HEALING RUNES

Because of their harmonious vibrations, runes have strong and powerful healing properties. If you have a complaint or illness, you can ask for a healing rune to be revealed to you while holding your rune bag. Next, pick out a single rune and either hold it in your hand and meditate with it or place it upon the ailing area. You will be amazed at how apt the message of the rune is to your ailment, and it often gives you guidance on the root cause and best treatment. For instance, if you draw the Is rune, it will help you to remove blockages in the body and get things moving; it also teaches the importance of contemplation. Drawing the Lagu rune will empower you to release emotional issues and to find balance and harmony; it also teaches the importance of eating a balanced diet of natural foods. It is vital that you learn the lessons that each illness is trying to teach.

All the runes have their individual healing properties and lessons to teach, for they are intrinsically linked. Illness is your body's way of telling you that you are doing something that is causing disharmony or "dis-ease" to the body. Your body is trying to teach you a lesson and as the runes also teach lessons, it follows that each lesson can represent an aspect of return to "ease" or health.

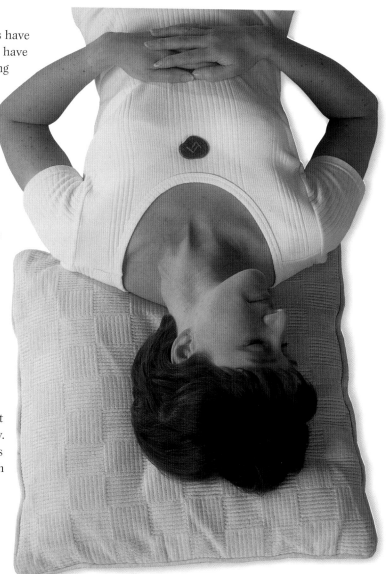

PLACE A RUNE UPON AN AILING AREA OF YOUR BODY TO GIVE YOU GUIDANCE ON YOUR AILMENT.

# HELPING OTHERS

ONCE YOU ARE FAMILIAR with the runes and the way they work, you can begin to help others by giving readings. Giving a reading for another person is the same as giving a reading for yourself, except that the other person draws the runes while you hold the intent in your mind of what each rune should represent. For example, if you are giving a reading using the three-rune spread, you would give the rune bag to the other person and ask them to draw out three runes, one at a time. As they draw out the first rune, you think, "I want this rune that they are drawing to comment upon the past". When they are drawing out the second rune,

you think, "I want this rune that they are drawing to comment upon the present" and so on.

Once the person has drawn their runes, take your rune bag back into your possession so that the vibration of the remaining runes can help empower you with the reading. Allow your intuition to speak to you and take note of what it says. You can then tie these intuitive insights in with the meaning of each rune.

With all such work, the more you do it, the better you become. It is probably best to begin by giving readings to family and friends before venturing into the realm of giving "cold" readings to people you do not know well.

ONCE YOU ARE FAMILIAR WITH THE RUNES, YOU CAN BEGIN TO HELP OTHERS BY GIVING THEM READINGS.

## HEALING OTHERS THROUGH THE FOUR ELEMENTS

Healing others is an extension of the four-element spread. Once a patient has drawn the four runes and received their interpretation, ask the patient to sit facing the direction in which they feel most comfortable. Place the four runes in position; north, south, east and west as they appeared in the four-element spread. Make a note of the direction in which the patient chooses to face; this will give you an indication of where they are on their spiritual path. If they sit facing north, you know that they are mainly dealing with the physical. If they sit facing west they are trying to balance their emotional side. If they sit facing south they are looking towards their destiny and if they sit facing east, they are seeking wisdom. If they sit facing one of the cross points (north-east, south-east, south-west or north-west) this indicates that they are trying to integrate two areas into their life, seeking balance and harmony between them.

While the patient is sitting within the four runes, you may wish to beat a drum or sing a song. The vibrations from the music will help to amplify the healing vibrations of the runes, as the patient sits and meditates in their chosen position. It is also good to get the patient to spend a few minutes at the end of the healing ceremony facing the opposite direction to their chosen one as this will help them to attract and integrate the energies of the other runes.

TO HEAL SOMEONE, ASK THEM TO SIT WITHIN THEIR FOUR CHOSEN RUNES, FACING THE DIRECTION IN WHICH THEY FEEL MOST COMFORTABLE.

# TOOLS AND TALISMANS

A S WELL AS BEING WORN about one's person, runes can also be used to empower magical tools. If you have a staff, wand or other magical tool that you wish to empower, you can ask the runes to show you which runes you need and then draw out as many as your intuition dictates. These can then be burnt, carved or painted on to your tool.

### BINDRUNES

Bindrunes consist of two or more runes bound together to form a single magical power symbol. Some examples of bindrunes are given below, but you can equally well create your own. All you need to do is to ask the runes to show you which ones to combine for your chosen purpose and then draw out as many runes as your intuition dictates.

RUNES ENGRAVED
ON A SWORD.

RUNES
CARVED
ON A STAFF.

THIS BINDRUNE MEANS "TO
GAIN INSPIRATION".

RUNES PAINTED
ON A WAND.

# RUNIC WISHING CEREMONY

IF YOU WRITE A WISH in runic script and then burn that script in the flame of a fire or candle, that wish will be sent out into the universe and will draw all the energies towards you to make that wish come true. Such wishing ceremonies have been used for thousands of years and are extremely powerful. Wishes can be for anything as long as they are not selfish and do not come from the ego. They can be written as single words, for example "Love", "Health" or "Togetherness", or as letters requesting specific wishes, for example "I ask that (person's name) be able to grow in inspiration and beauty".

Once you have written your wish on the paper, seal it with a rune; this can be done by drawing a single rune from the bag and writing it upon the folded paper. As you watch your wish burn, visualize its energy travelling to every corner of the universe, sending a message that will attract all the right energies you need to make that wish come true. After performing your wishing ceremony, always remember that everything that comes to you throughout your journey in life comes to teach you, and is a stepping stone taking you closer to the realization of that wish.

1 Write a wish on a piece of paper in runic script. It can be a single word or a simple message. Seal the wish with a rune.

2 Cast your wish into the fire, and focus on its energy travelling to every corner of the universe.

WISHES CAN ALSO BE BURNT OVER A CANDLE FLAME DURING A WISHING CEREMONY.

# RUNES AND THEIR MEANINGS

# FEOH RUNE

**FEOH**
CORRESPONDING LETTER: F
RUNE: ᚠ
MEANING: CATTLE
DIVINATORY MEANING:
SPIRITUAL RICHNESS

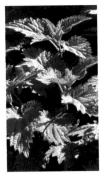

**ASSOCIATIONS:**
TREE: ELDER
COLOUR: LIGHT RED
HERB: NETTLE
GEMSTONE: MOSS AGATE

### INTERPRETATION OF RUNE

Feoh speaks of a spiritual richness that is to be used for the benefit of all. It is a rune of unselfish abundance. Let your richness shine forth to lighten your path and the paths of others. You will never run out of your spiritual richness although you should not waste it on those who will abuse it; discernment is important.

*"Wealth should never be hoarded but should be used for the benefit of all."*

### INTERPRETATION OF REVERSED RUNE

You have great richness within you, but its light is masked by emotional imbalances. Strive for balance in your life and you will discover the rich wealth of gifts and talents that are already yours. Claim your destiny.

### MEANING: CATTLE

To the Nordic people, cattle were a sign of status and wealth. Like all animals, cattle were sacred but they were also feasted upon at times of celebration, showing that wealth should be used for the benefit of all. While physical wealth is transient, spiritual wealth is permanent. The wisdom that you learn and integrate into your life can never be taken away from you, no matter how many times you share that wisdom. Everyone has spiritual gifts, and if you are unaware of your gifts it does not mean that you have none; on the contrary, it means that you have not yet uncovered them. For example, having the capacity for compassion is a sharing of the gift of love. Each person has many gifts; once they are recognized, they can be used.

# UR RUNE

UR
CORRESPONDING LETTER: U
RUNE: ᚢ
MEANING: AUROCH
DIVINATORY MEANING:
STRENGTH

ASSOCIATIONS:
TREE: BIRCH
COLOUR: DARK GREEN
HERB: SPHAGNUM MOSS
GEMSTONE: CARBUNCLE

## INTERPRETATION OF RUNE

You have the strength within you to fulfil all your dreams, but with that strength comes responsibility. Strength is not a force with which to exert power over others, but a force to stop others exerting power over you. Use your strength to keep you focused on your path, to stop yourself being off-balanced by others. There are always some people who are negative. Strength comes from not letting those people upset you and this in turn comes from mastering the ego.

*"To find your true strength, you must first face your weaknesses."*

## INTERPRETATION OF REVERSED RUNE

To be strong, you must first know weakness. Look honestly within yourself without fear, knowing that once you recognize those areas of weakness, you will be able to work on them to turn them into strengths.

### MEANING: AUROCH

Aurochs were wild oxen and a powerful totemic animal of the Nordic tradition symbolizing strength. Nowadays, strength is greatly misunderstood. Many people equate strength with dominance and inflexibility. They also confuse pride with strength, whereas pride is actually a weakness created by the ego. True strength only comes once the ego is mastered. To find your true strength, you must first face your weaknesses. Once you recognize where your weaknesses lie, you can then turn them into strengths. This process can be frightening for many people and there are those who try to hide their weaknesses rather than facing up to them.

# THORN RUNE

THORN
CORRESPONDING LETTER: TH
RUNE: Þ
MEANING: THORN
DIVINATORY MEANING:
SPIRITUAL AUTHORITY

ASSOCIATIONS:
TREE: THORN/OAK
COLOUR: BRIGHT RED
HERB: HOUSELEEK
GEMSTONE: SAPPHIRE

## INTERPRETATION OF RUNE

You have the power within you to face anything that might cross your path. Fear nothing, for you have the authority to claim your destiny. Let no one deter you from your search for the truth. Hold fast to your birthright, be a spiritual being, but always remember to keep your feet firmly on the ground. Spiritual authority brings power and it is up to you to use that power in an unselfish and loving way. Power can corrupt if you do not have a true and honest heart. You should never need to tell others of your authority; knowing that you have it should be enough. To utilize the power of this rune fully, you must first master the ego. Spiritual authority, like strength, is a power that is designed to help you keep on your path and not a power to exert over others for selfish ends.

*"You have the power within you to face anything that might cross your path."*

### MEANING: THORN

The shamans and magicians of northern Europe have long associated the thorn trees with spiritual authority. Blackthorn was greatly favoured as the material for making staffs and powerful wands. Thorn trees are symbolic of protection and their wood was often used to make talismans to ward off evil. The protection that comes from the thorn tree is the protection of spiritual authority, and gives you the power to stand up for the truth when surrounded by lies, and to claim the spiritual path that is your birthright. The blackthorn has a sister tree, the hawthorn, which, while being a powerful protective tree like the blackthorn, also has soothing and balancing feminine energies.

# ANSUR RUNE

ANSUR
CORRESPONDING LETTER: A
RUNE: ᚠ
MEANING: A MOUTH
DIVINATORY MEANING:
A MESSAGE

ASSOCIATIONS:
TREE: ASH
COLOUR: DARK BLUE
HERB: FLY AGARIC
GEMSTONE: EMERALD

## INTERPRETATION OF RUNE

The answers to your questions are already here: you have just not heard them yet. Look for signs and confirmations which are all around you. Everything has significance. If you learn this truth, you will understand the messages around you. Check that you are not ignoring the message because you do not like its contents. Trust that everything that comes to you comes to teach you, and that by acknowledging the truth you will grow in knowledge and wisdom.

*"Everything that comes to you comes to teach you."*

## INTERPRETATION OF REVERSED RUNE

You have not found answers because you are asking the wrong questions. Seek in a different way; look within and all will become clear.

### MEANING: MOUTH

In the Nordic tradition, the mouth is symbolic of communication. Messages come in many forms and communication problems arise from an inability to decipher these messages correctly. A word can have completely different meanings to different people. For instance, to someone brought up in northern Europe, the word "seaside" creates a picture of sand, seaweed, donkey rides and ice cream. To someone brought up in the Caribbean, however, the same word creates a picture of palm trees, clear blue water, azure skies, beautiful fish and corals, scorching sun and, perhaps, storms and hurricanes. The same word can create two very dramatically different pictures.

# RAD RUNE

RAD
CORRESPONDING LETTER: R
RUNE: **R**
MEANING: A CARTWHEEL
DIVINATORY MEANING:
THE WHEEL OF LIFE

ASSOCIATIONS:
TREE: OAK
COLOUR: BRIGHT RED
HERB: MUGWORT
GEMSTONE: CHRYSOPRASE

## INTERPRETATION OF RUNE

Recognize that everything comes in cycles and that by following these cycles, you will be able to progress quickly and efficiently. Align yourself to the seasons by eating seasonal foods and honouring the turning of the year. Embrace hard times in the certainty that the harder it is now, the more beautiful things will be in the future. Everything has its opposite, and challenges bring equal and opposite rewards.

*"When times are difficult, be assured that they will not go on forever."*

## INTERPRETATION OF REVERSED RUNE

Stop trying to resist the inevitable. Your path is set out before you; tread it without fear. Take one step at a time and you will soon find yourself "flowing" once more.

### MEANING: CARTWHEEL

Life is a journey along which we encounter challenges that give us opportunities to learn lessons. Everything in life is cyclical. All things have a beginning, a middle and an end. Once you recognize this fact, you can "go with the flow" and let things unfold rather than always resisting. All journeys and lessons have a beginning, a middle and an end. When times are difficult, be assured that they will not go on forever. Once you have learnt the lessons that the hard times are trying to teach you, you will no longer need to suffer them. Every situation is a potential lesson. The faster you learn, the quicker you will progress, so embrace everything with pleasure, in the knowledge that there are lessons to be learnt.

# KEN RUNE

<u>KEN</u>
CORRESPONDING LETTER: K
RUNE: ⟨
MEANING: A TORCH
DIVINATORY MEANING:
ENLIGHTENMENT

## INTERPRETATION OF RUNE

You are coming into a new understanding of life and its meaning. New insights await you but this is not a time for complacency. You must use this new understanding or it will be worthless to you. Always look for ways in which you can use your insights for the good of yourself and others. Enlightenment is like a jug of fine wine: it must be poured out before it can be refilled. Do not be fooled into thinking that enlightenment is your goal in life, it is not. It is the starting point of an adventure of learning that, if followed with a true heart, will show you great wisdom and understanding.

<u>ASSOCIATIONS:</u>
TREE: PINE
COLOUR: LIGHT RED
HERB: COWSLIP
GEMSTONE: BLOODSTONE

*"Enlightenment needs to be tempered with wisdom before its true worth and power can be known."*

## MEANING: A TORCH

Illumination allows one to see in the dark. Enlightenment is a spiritual illumination. It is coming into a new understanding, like opening your eyes for the first time or like turning on a light. You are not seeing anything new – it has always been there – you are just seeing it for the first time. Enlightenment is a beginning, not an end. This new understanding needs to be utilized and tempered with wisdom before its true worth and power can be known. With knowledge comes responsibility, because greater knowledge leads to greater power. It is vital that you use your knowledge and power only for what is good and right.

# GEOFU RUNE

GEOFU
CORRESPONDING LETTER: G
RUNE: X
MEANING: A GIFT
DIVINATORY MEANING:
A SPIRITUAL GIFT

### INTERPRETATION OF RUNE

A gift is coming to you and this presents you with a choice. You can either accept it or reject it. If you choose to accept it, you must be prepared to give in return. Everything has its price, but with spiritual gifts the cost is always worth it in the end. It is up to you to find the balance between giving and receiving and to learn the lesson of responsible giving. You must learn when to give and who to give to. It is not appropriate to give to everyone indiscriminately for there are those who do not wish to receive, so giving to them is a waste of energy and an abuse of your own gifts.

ASSOCIATIONS:
TREE: ASH/ELM
COLOUR: DEEP BLUE
HERB: HEARTSEASE
GEMSTONE: OPAL

*"To tread a spiritual path, you must be both a giver and a receiver."*

### MEANING: A GIFT

To receive a gift, you must also be a giver. Likewise, if you give, you must be willing to receive. The cycle of giving and receiving must never be broken. Those who take without giving on a physical or emotional level lose their own spiritual gifts. To tread a spiritual path, you must be both a giver and a receiver. To be truly balanced you must be able to receive a gift with total humility, knowing that if you abuse a spiritual gift, you will lose it. Compassion is a sharing of the gift of love and understanding. Encouragement is the sharing of the gift of empowerment. Each person has many gifts; once they are recognized, they can be used.

# WYNN RUNE

WYNN
CORRESPONDING LETTER: W
RUNE: ᛈ
MEANING: HAPPINESS
DIVINATORY MEANING:
BALANCE

## INTERPRETATION OF RUNE

Happiness is yours if you are willing to work for it. You must strive for balance and harmony in your life. Always be looking for solutions rather than dwelling upon problems. For happiness to last, it needs to be founded upon truth and honesty. Hide from the truth and you shall never see true happiness. Seek only what is good and right, and good fortune cannot fail to follow.

*"To have happiness, you must be at peace with yourself."*

ASSOCIATIONS:
TREE: ASH
COLOUR: YELLOW
HERB: FLAX
GEMSTONE: DIAMOND

## INTERPRETATION OF REVERSED RUNE

The happiness you seek is already yours, but your attachment to the past is preventing you from seeing it. It is time to let go of the old and embrace the new.

### MEANING: HAPPINESS

True happiness only comes to those who are balanced. Happiness is found within and is not dependent on any other person or thing. To have happiness, you must be at peace with yourself and with your place in life. This requires you to eat, think and act in a balanced manner. Healthy eating (fresh, natural, organic, unrefined foods) is fundamental to health and happiness and will naturally lead to healthy thoughts and actions. So seek balance and harmony within, and you will attract peace and happiness for yourself. Happiness comes from seeking and finding the truth, then integrating it into every aspect of your life.

# HAGALL RUNE

HAGALL
CORRESPONDING LETTER: H
RUNE: ᚼ
MEANING: HAIL
DIVINATORY MEANING:
A CHALLENGE

### INTERPRETATION OF RUNE

Challenges are occurring in your life. These are not to be feared, but to be embraced. A hailstorm may seem daunting, but if you catch a hailstone you will realize that it is only water and nothing to be feared. So it is with challenges. Grit your teeth, fire up your determination, and face the challenges head-on in the assurance that they are just stepping stones to the realization of your dream. Every challenge comes to teach. Remember, the greater the challenge, potentially the more wisdom you can acquire once you have overcome the obstacles in your path.

ASSOCIATIONS:
TREE: ASH/YEW
COLOUR: LIGHT BLUE
HERB: LILY-OF-THE-VALLEY
GEMSTONE: ONYX

*"Never shy away from challenges as they strengthen and teach you throughout your life."*

### MEANING: HAIL

Challenges occur to teach you and you should never shy away from them. When you fix in your mind a vision of how you would like your future to be, you send energy in the form of thought waves out into the universe. These vibrations then attract to you all the things that need to be in place before that dream can become reality. You cannot know all the lessons, but if you stay fixed on your dream, be assured that you will be attracting all the lessons you need. When life becomes difficult, it is not a sign to abandon your dream, it is merely a stepping stone to the realization of that dream. It is an opportunity to learn lessons that you will need when your dream becomes reality. Face the challenge – when you have overcome it, you will be stronger and wiser.

# NIED RUNE

NIED
CORRESPONDING LETTER: N
RUNE: ᚾ
MEANING: NEED
DIVINATORY MEANING:
NEED

ASSOCIATIONS:
TREE: BEECH
COLOUR: BLACK
HERB: BISTORT
GEMSTONE: LAPIS LAZULI

## INTERPRETATION OF RUNE

You are getting exactly what you need at this moment to allow you to make the best progress on your spiritual path. Everything is how it is meant to be. It may appear to be the very opposite of what you want, but this state is not permanent, it is merely a series of lessons that must be learnt so that you can make the transition from negative to positive. You need to have total acceptance of what has happened in the past, to keep your mind fixed on where you want to be, while trusting that everything in the present is meant to be there and is to be learnt from. The past is just a memory, the future just a dream, the present is the only place where you can have influence; it is the place in which you exist.

*"To achieve your wants, you often need to experience the very opposite of your wants."*

### MEANING: NEED

What we want and what we need in our lives are often two completely different things. If you want to be strong, you will need to examine your weaknesses closely. This creates a paradox. You have a vision of being strong, and yet all you see are weaknesses. It is only when you realize that the weaknesses need to be faced and turned to strengths, that you will begin to understand the difference between wants and needs. To achieve your wants, you often need to experience the very opposite of your wants. To be strong, you must first experience weakness; to find your path, you must first lose it; to be beautiful within, you must first face up to and deal with your ugly inner side.

IS
CORRESPONDING LETTER: I
RUNE: \
MEANING: ICE
DIVINATORY MEANING:
STANDSTILL

ASSOCIATIONS:
TREE: ALDER
COLOUR: BLACK
HERB: HENBANE
GEMSTONE: CAT'S-EYE

# IS RUNE

### INTERPRETATION OF RUNE

Things appear to be at a standstill and this is not a time to try to force movement. Patience and wisdom are called for: patience because you will have to wait until things change externally before you can proceed; and wisdom because you need to decide how best to use your waiting time. This is not the time to be abandoning your dreams; on the contrary, this is an opportunity for you to reaffirm them. This is a time for contemplation and preparation, not for depression and regrets. Be assured that things will change as surely as winter changes to spring and then to summer.

*"When life seems at a standstill, review the past and look to the future."*

### MEANING: ICE

Ice can form an impenetrable barrier. The only thing you can do is to wait for the thaw. But winter is not a time for idleness; there is much that can be done in preparation for the thaw. Although nothing appears to be moving, everything must be in place and ready if you are to take full advantage of the coming thaw. Winter is also a time of contemplation, a time to review the past, to assimilate all the lessons that the past has taught, and a time to look to the future and reaffirm your dreams. Recognize that the time you are in is just another phase of your unfolding path of learning; when this phase is over, a new one will begin. Use this time to rest a while; you will need to focus all your energies for what is to come.

# JARA RUNE

## INTERPRETATION OF RUNE

This is a time of reaping rewards from the seeds sown in the past. It is a time of plenty, a time of joy and celebration. But it is also a time of great work with no time for complacency. The harvest does not last forever. The winter of more hard lessons lies ahead and you would do well to make sure that you have stored enough knowledge and wisdom to face your next challenges. This is another turning point in your life, not your goal. There are greater harvests for you to experience in the future, but before any harvest there has to be preparation of the land, sowing of the seed, tending of the seedlings and support of the forming fruits.

JARA
CORRESPONDING LETTER: J
RUNE:
MEANING: HARVEST
DIVINATORY MEANING:
HARVEST

ASSOCIATIONS:
TREE: OAK
COLOUR: LIGHT BLUE
HERB: ROSEMARY
GEMSTONE: CORNELIAN

*"This is a time of hard work, and of reaping rewards for past efforts."*

## MEANING: HARVEST

Harvest is the time of hardest work. The fruits of man's labour must be collected and stored if they are not to spoil. It is a time of preparation. Everything must be in its place before the first snows of winter come. If the winter is to be survived, it is imperative that as much grain and produce as possible is stored. Nothing must be missed and everything must be done correctly. If grains are not stored in the right way, they will rot and spoil long before the winter is over. This is certainly not a time to be resting on your laurels. The harvest feasting takes place only after the harvest is finished, not before. You are at the end of a cycle, but remember that endings only lead to new beginnings.

# EOH RUNE

EOH
CORRESPONDING LETTER: Y
RUNE: ᛇ
MEANING: A YEW TREE
DIVINATORY MEANING:
TRANSFORMATION

### INTERPRETATION OF RUNE

This is a time of transformation; a time to let go of the old and embrace the new. It is a time of death, the dying of the past, and yet it is also a time of new beginnings, new life and new dreams. The only constant is change, and if you want to make quick and efficient progress on your path, you have to learn to embrace change instead of resisting it. To resist change is to risk stagnation, to risk becoming stuck at the point of spiritual death instead of walking forwards towards the new birth. Do not be afraid; change is scary, but if you remain true to yourself and keep to your path, you will soon find yourself basking in the fresh sun of new enlightenments.

ASSOCIATIONS:
TREE: YEW
COLOUR: DARK BLUE
HERB: MANDRAKE
GEMSTONE: TOPAZ

*"By embracing change, you will make quick progress on your spiritual path."*

### MEANING: YEW TREE

The yew tree has a long association with immortality and the cycle of death and rebirth. As a yew tree grows, its central trunk becomes soft and starts to decay. While this occurs, a new sapling begins to grow within the tree. When the tree matures, the same process continues to occur until the tree is made up of many trees growing from the centre outwards. This amazing regeneration is what enables a yew tree to grow to an immense size and age. A yew tree is said to have known many lives and so can help you remember past lives. Because of its longevity, the yew is also an ancient wisdom keeper.

# Peorth Rune

PEORTH
CORRESPONDING LETTER: P
RUNE: ᛈ
MEANING: A DICE CUP
DIVINATORY MEANING:
CHOICE

ASSOCIATIONS:
TREE: BEECH
COLOUR: BLACK
HERB: ACONITE
GEMSTONE: AQUAMARINE

## INTERPRETATION OF RUNE

You always have a choice in everything. No one can upset you, you can only choose to be upset. No one can exert power over you unless you choose to allow them to. Claim your power of choice. Do not allow others to compromise your truth and do not let others prevent you from doing what you need to do. The only danger here is not to make a choice, to leave things to fate. That path will only disempower you.

*"Make your own choices and take charge of your own destiny."*

## INTERPRETATION OF REVERSED RUNE

The dice have been rolled and fate has control of your life, but it does not have to be this way. You can regain power. Start to make choices for yourself instead of following the choices of others.

### MEANING: A DICE CUP

The dice cup is the receptacle from which dice are thrown; it is the source of chance or fate. A die which is not thrown is just a lump of wood with dots on it. It is only when the dice are thrown that they have significance, because the manner and position of their falling is in the hands of fate. People think of fate as an inevitable tide, but it is not. Fate merely presents you with choices. There is the choice of whether or not to throw the dice and whether to heed what the dice say. Life is full of choices, but many people choose to let the hand of fate guide them instead of taking charge of their destiny and claiming it in spite of what fate may bring.

# Elhaz Rune

ELHAZ
CORRESPONDING LETTER: Z
RUNE: ᛉ
MEANING: AN ELK
DIVINATORY MEANING:
PROTECTION

ASSOCIATIONS:
TREE: YEW
COLOUR: GOLD
HERB: ANGELICA
GEMSTONE: AMETHYST

## INTERPRETATION OF RUNE

Be assured that although your path ahead is fraught with dangers, you need have no fear for you have the power of protection within you. You will be safe as long as you do not act recklessly. This is a favourable time for risky ventures, although all things must be built on firm foundations. Do not become complacent.

*"Although your path is fraught with danger, you have the power of protection within you."*

## INTERPRETATION OF REVERSED RUNE

Proceed with caution and do not act in haste. You are vulnerable to hostile influences and need to concentrate on building your strength physically, emotionally and spiritually before pressing forwards.

## MEANING: AN ELK

To the Nordic people, the elk was a powerful totemic animal with very strong protective energies. The wearing of this rune is said to guard the wearer against all manner of attacks and dangers, both physical and psychic. The rune is said to represent the elk when the animal is viewed face on. The antlers of the elk were also thought of as psychic receivers which could pick up the subtle vibrations of all living things around. The protective energies of the elk come not only from its ability to sense danger, but also its speed and the skill with which it flees dangerous situations quickly and efficiently. Therefore, the Elhaz rune is a powerful ally to help you to find a safe passage through difficult times.

SIGEL
CORRESPONDING LETTER: S
RUNE: ᛋ
MEANING: THE SUN
DIVINATORY MEANING:
GOOD FORTUNE

ASSOCIATIONS:
TREE: JUNIPER
COLOUR: WHITE/SILVER
HERB: MISTLETOE
GEMSTONE: RUBY

# SIGEL RUNE

## INTERPRETATION OF RUNE

You have the power to bring things to fruition. Good fortune awaits you and there is a positive feel to everything. This is not a time to rest and relax, however, rather it is an ideal time to look within at the darker aspects of your nature. The power of the sun will enable you to face those dark parts of your being without fear and finally to gain power over them. This is a good time to seek solutions to problems as they are all within your grasp.

*"You have the power to bring things to fruition."*

## MEANING: THE SUN

To the Nordic people, the sun was considered the giver of life, for without its rays there would be no food and sustenance. The sun is associated with all that is good, just and right. The light of the sun banishes darkness and rejuvenates the spirit. It is also the "destroyer of ice", as one Icelandic runic poem describes it, and is therefore a powerful rune to counteract the negative aspects of the Is rune. Sigel is also a rune of truth; the power of light illuminates the darkness of deception, giving clarity of thought and vision. It will show you not only deception in others, but within you. It will shine a light upon the path of all who hold it.

# TYR RUNE

TYR
CORRESPONDING LETTER: T
RUNE: ↑
MEANING: TYR
(THE WARRIOR GOD)
DIVINATORY MEANING:
INITIATION

ASSOCIATIONS:
TREE: OAK
COLOUR: BRIGHT RED
HERB: SAGE
GEMSTONE: CORAL

## INTERPRETATION OF RUNE

This rune symbolizes new challenges and initiations into new understandings. There is a need for fearlessness, for your victory is already assured if your heart remains true. This is a time to make use of all the skills and wisdom that you have learnt so far. Protect your faith, as it will be challenged, but the truth will always be victorious in the end.

*"Now is the time to make use of all the skills and wisdom that you have learnt so far."*

## INTERPRETATION OF REVERSED RUNE

You have all the powers you need for the challenges ahead but you need to unlock your true potential. Do not let fear stand in your way. Look honestly at your weaknesses and resolve to turn them into strengths. The warrior is within you and it is now time to let that energy come forth.

### MEANING: TYR (THE WARRIOR GOD)

The path of the warrior presents challenges and initiations. The warrior must learn many skills including patience, keenness of sense, speed and agility. He must be of a good and strong heart, with a firm belief in the sacredness of that which he protects. As a companion, one could not wish for a better ally, for the warrior has a natural instinct to protect and survive. He is always resourceful and focuses on solutions rather than problems. The wise warrior knows that mistakes are not failures, but rather lessons to be learnt if one is honest and humble enough to seek. The man who makes no mistakes in his life becomes an old fool.

# BEORC RUNE

BEORC
CORRESPONDING LETTER: B
RUNE: ᛒ
MEANING: A BIRCH TREE
DIVINATORY MEANING:
NEW BEGINNINGS

ASSOCIATIONS:
TREE: BIRCH
COLOUR: DARK GREEN
HERB: LADY'S MANTLE
GEMSTONE: MOONSTONE

## INTERPRETATION OF RUNE

This is an exciting time of new beginnings and fresh adventures, a time of great activity and energy. This is a time to sow seeds, but remember that the harvest is still a long way off; do not expect to see immediate rewards for your efforts, as new ideas need nurturing and feeding before they will bear fruit. This is a time to make sure that the past is truly put in its place. If one has learnt all the lessons that the past has had to teach, it need never be revisited. It can be left behind and one can venture forth with boldness to embrace new pastures. This is also a good time to think about a spiritual spring cleaning, clearing away the old to make way for the new.

*"This is an exciting time of new beginnings and fresh adventures."*

## MEANING: A BIRCH TREE

The birch tree is a pioneer tree. When forest or scrub land is destroyed by fire, the birch is one of the first trees to re-colonize the land. It is symbolic of birth and new beginnings, like the phoenix rising from the ashes. Magically, the birch tree has long been associated with purification. The birch broom was used to sweep negativity from a house, while the punishment of "birching" was said to drive evil from criminals. The old pagan ritual of beating the bounds to mark land boundaries and to cleanse negativity from the soil also utilized birch. This ancient practice is still performed in remote regions of Scandinavia and the British Isles.

EHWAZ
CORRESPONDING LETTER: E
RUNE: M
MEANING: A HORSE
DIVINATORY MEANING:
PROGRESS

ASSOCIATIONS:
TREE: OAK/ASH
COLOUR: WHITE
HERB: RAGWORT
GEMSTONE: ICELAND SPAR

# EHWAZ RUNE

## INTERPRETATION OF RUNE

You have the support to be able to make swift progress along your path, but this is dependent upon you being as loyal and supportive to those around you as they are to you. The horse is a proud animal but it does not let its pride get in the way of its purpose. In the same way, you should always be proud of your achievements while remaining outwardly humble to ensure your travels will be swift and sure.

*"Always be as loyal and supportive to those around you as they are to you."*

## INTERPRETATION OF REVERSED RUNE

You need to make new connections. This will draw the energies towards you that will help you overcome all obstacles. Seek out those who share your attitude, knowing that everyone who enters your life has lessons to teach you.

MEANING: A HORSE

The horse was regarded as a sacred animal throughout the old world and is recorded in many myths and legends as a faithful and loyal ally. The energy of the horse is powerful and primal. It allows you to see the world from a higher perspective, helping you to avoid obstacles and to make swift progress along your path. The horse is also associated with fire, the element of free expression and unfolding destiny. The energy of the horse can help to clear stagnation and remove blocks, both internal and external. This makes it a valuable ally on the spiritual path. Because the only constant is change, stagnation should have no place upon a spiritual path. Ehwaz helps one to seek to make progress on the adventurous path of our destiny.

# MANN RUNE

MANN
CORRESPONDING LETTER: M
RUNE: ᛗ
MEANING: A HUMAN
DIVINATORY MEANING:
DESTINY

ASSOCIATIONS:
TREE: HOLLY
COLOUR: DEEP RED
HERB: MADDER
GEMSTONE: GARNET

### INTERPRETATION OF RUNE

Your destiny awaits you, so claim it. For you to be a spiritual being, you must be balanced in body, mind and spirit. Embrace everything – good and bad – with total acceptance and pleasure, secure in the knowledge that everything that comes to you is there to teach. By learning each lesson as it presents itself, you will go onwards and upwards.

*"The path of destiny is a path of growth and fulfilment."*

### INTERPRETATION OF REVERSED RUNE

The path of destiny seems hard, but as you tread it, you become wiser and stronger. Have faith – you have the strength and power to deal with all of life's problems and to make choices as long as you are willing to learn. Do not let your own ego, or those of others, fill your mind with misgivings.

### MEANING: A HUMAN

Every human being has a destiny and it is every human being's right to fulfil that destiny. Destiny is all about choice. You can choose to take responsibility for your life, to be a spiritual being and to fulfil your destiny, or you can choose to drift along with whatever life throws at you.

The path of destiny is not an easy path, for it holds many lessons and challenges along the way, but it is a path of growth and fulfilment. The other path appears easier, but it is filled with ill-health and dissatisfaction.

# LAGU RUNE

LAGU
CORRESPONDING LETTER: L
RUNE: ↑
MEANING: WATER, SEA
DIVINATORY MEANING:
ATTUNEMENT TO
CREATION

ASSOCIATIONS:
TREE: WILLOW
COLOUR: DEEP GREEN
HERB: LEEK
GEMSTONE: PEARL

## INTERPRETATION OF RUNE

It is only by attunement to creation that your life will truly flow as it is meant to. Emotional balance comes from eating in balance with creation around you. Natural foods lead to natural flow, whereas unnatural foods lead to disharmony and stagnation. The sea is always fluid and moving, so it should be a part of your life. Embrace change, for it is the only constant in life.

*"Being in harmony with creation gives you emotional balance."*

## INTERPRETATION OF REVERSED RUNE

You need to learn to go with the flow. There is a need to initiate some movement into many areas of your life or you will start to become stagnant. A few, simple changes can bring about great, positive effects.

### MEANING: WATER, SEA

Water is a primal power that can never be truly contained or controlled. Water flows where it will, drawn back and forth by the power of the moon. All fluids on the earth are governed in just the same way by the moon. This includes the sea, the fluid within plants and the fluids within you. To be in harmony with creation, you need to attune yourself to the seasons and the moon. Eating and living in harmony with nature around you gives you a new perspective and opens up many possibilities to acquire new and greater knowledge and transform it into wisdom.

# ING RUNE

ING
CORRESPONDING LETTER: NG
RUNE: ◇
MEANING: ING (THE
FERTILITY GOD)
DIVINATORY MEANING:
THE FIRE WITHIN

ASSOCIATIONS:
TREE: APPLE
COLOUR: YELLOW
HERB: SELF-HEAL
GEMSTONE: AMBER

## INTERPRETATION OF RUNE

You are on a spiritual path and although you may feel isolated at times, you can be safe in the knowledge that within you burns the fire of inspiration which urges you ever onwards and upwards. Feed the fire by always striving to learn more, never resting in the illusion of complacency. Seek only answers and never become waylaid with too many questions. Live one day at a time, knowing that the past is just a memory, the future just a dream, and the here and now is what matters.

*"The fire of inspiration urges you to keep striving towards spiritual fulfilment."*

### MEANING: ING
### (THE FERTILITY GOD)

Ing symbolizes the spark of creation, the power to give life and to make the land fertile. It is the fire within everyone that drives them forwards and keeps them striving towards spiritual fulfilment; it is the power to keep going when things get tough. This fire can lie dormant for many years, but when it is fuelled by the breath of acknowledgement, by its existence being recognized, it is almost impossible to extinguish. Ing teaches that you cannot change the past; the present is the only place where you can truly have influence. Ing helps you to let the past go, and keeps your eyes on your dream, while you live and work in the here and now.

# DAEG RUNE

DAEG
CORRESPONDING LETTER: D
RUNE: ᛗ
MEANING: DAY (LIGHT)
DIVINATORY MEANING:
THE LIGHT

ASSOCIATIONS:
TREE: SPRUCE
COLOUR: LIGHT BLUE
HERB: CLARY
GEMSTONE: DIAMOND

## INTERPRETATION OF RUNE

The power of the light shines before you, guiding you clearly upon your path. As long as you remain true, only good fortune can come your way. You need have no fear, for you are well protected by the power of the light. The light will give you clear vision so that you may see and avoid dangers before they enter your life. The only warning is against being blinded, although it is not the light that will blind you, but your ego. The ego, if not mastered, will allow your success to blind you, so always remain humble and thankful for all the good things that come to you.

*"As long as you remain true, only good fortune can come your way."*

### MEANING: DAY (LIGHT)

Daeg is the rune of midday and midsummer. It represents the positive energy of light at its most potent and powerful and is therefore a rune of great protection when painted over doorways and on window shutters. Daeg is positivity at its strongest, signifying success, growth, progress, clarity of vision and protection against harmful influences. It allows you to see the positive within every negative. Daeg also helps you remember that everything is given to you. If you do not use these gifts with love and beauty, they will be taken from you. You own nothing; everything is lent to you by the creator, so always use your gifts with respect and wisdom.

# OTHEL RUNE

OTHEL
CORRESPONDING LETTER: O
RUNE: ᛟ
MEANING: A POSSESSION
DIVINATORY MEANING:
FOCUS AND FREEDOM

ASSOCIATIONS:
TREE: HAWTHORN
COLOUR: DEEP YELLOW
HERB: CLOVER
GEMSTONE: RUBY

### INTERPRETATION OF RUNE

This is a time to re-focus. Fix your dream firmly in your mind, trusting that your thoughts will attract the energies that you need to make that dream reality. Concentration is needed if you are to read all the signs that are appearing before you. Allow whatever must happen to proceed unhindered. Do not try to force issues. Your dream is like a dove sitting on the palm of your hand. If you try to possess it or to keep hold of it, you risk killing it.

*"Focus your thoughts to attract the right energies that you need to make your dream reality."*

### INTERPRETATION OF REVERSED RUNE

If you try to own something, you will risk losing it. Allow everything and everyone to be. If you do not like something, you can only change by initiating change within yourself.

### MEANING: A POSSESSION

Othel is the rune into which energies can be concentrated and focused. It has an image of an enclosure of land or of a magical circle. Although Othel means "a possession", it is in the sense of holding rather than owning. We own nothing; all things are merely loaned to us, including our bodies. For the power of Othel to be experienced, you need to be able to concentrate and relax at the same time. Focus on a thought, then wait patiently for other energies to be attracted to it. Never try to force things, but always keep in mind where you want to go. The energy of this thought will direct and guide you in the right direction. Never lose sight of your dream.

# A FINAL WORD

As YOU WILL HAVE REALIZED through reading this book, life is a series of lessons. The quicker you learn, the more progress you can make upon your spiritual path. We are all spiritual beings and everything we experience presents us with an opportunity to learn. To be free, happy and fulfilled requires that we let go of the past, having learnt all we can from it, look forward to the future by holding on to our dreams, and live in the present. We can neither change the past nor predict the future; we can only have influence in the present.

You cannot change others, you can only change yourself. But it is by changing yourself that you influence others to change. Always be looking for ways to learn and improve yourself. Embrace change and accept everything that comes to you with pleasure, firm in the knowledge that everything has a beginning, a middle and an end. Even hard times can become good times because they are opportunities for learning. Accept these opportunities and turn them to your advantage.

If someone is unpleasant to you, rather than being riddled with thoughts of anger, unforgiveness and revenge, seek out the lesson. Ask yourself, "What is this experience trying to teach me?" Once you have learnt the lesson, you will be able to go to that person and say "Thank you for being unpleasant to me, because your negative behaviour has taught me a great lesson which has made me a better and wiser person." The question of forgiveness does not arise because the person has actually done you a great favour. If you can really live this way, no one will have power over you and life will become a continual adventure full of lessons and wisdom.

May the sun light your path, may love surround you and may the light of inspiration always burn strong within you.

## TABLE OF CORRESPONDENCIES

| LETTER | SIGN | NAME | MEANING | TREE | COLOUR | HERB | GEMSTONE |
|---|---|---|---|---|---|---|---|
| F | | Feoh | Cattle | Elder | Light red | Nettle | Moss agate |
| U | | Ur | Auroch | Birch | Dark green | Sphagnum moss | Carbuncle |
| TH | | Thorn | Thorn | Thorn/oak | Bright red | Houseleek | Sapphire |
| A | | Ansur | A mouth | Ash | Dark blue | Fly agaric | Emerald |
| R | | Rad | A cartwheel | Oak | Bright red | Mugwort | Chrysoprase |
| K | | Ken | A torch | Pine | Light red | Cowslip | Bloodstone |
| G | | Geofu | A gift | Ash/elm | Deep blue | Heartsease | Opal |
| W | | Wynn | Happiness | Ash | Yellow | Flax | Diamond |
| H | | Hagall | Hail | Ash/yew | Light blue | Lily-of-the-valley | Onyx |
| N | | Nied | Need | Beech | Black | Bistort | Lapis lazuli |
| I | | Is | Ice | Alder | Black | Henbane | Cat's-eye |
| J | | Jara | Harvest | Oak | Light blue | Rosemary | Cornelian |
| Y | | Eoh | A yew tree | Yew | Dark blue | Mandrake | Topaz |
| P | | Peorth | A dice cup | Beech | Black | Aconite | Aquamarine |
| Z | | Elhaz | An elk | Yew | Gold | Angelica | Amethyst |
| S | | Sigel | The sun | Juniper | White/silver | Mistletoe | Ruby |
| T | | Tyr | The god Tyr | Oak | Bright red | Sage | Coral |
| B | | Beorc | A birch tree | Birch | Dark green | Lady's mantle | Moonstone |
| E | | Ehwaz | A horse | Oak/ash | White | Ragwort | Iceland spar |
| M | | Mann | A human | Holly | Deep red | Madder | Garnet |
| L | | Lagu | Water, sea | Willow | Deep green | Leek | Pearl |
| NG | | Ing | The god Ing | Apple | Yellow | Self-heal | Amber |
| D | | Daeg | Day (light) | Spruce | Light blue | Clary | Diamond |
| O | | Othel | A possession | Hawthorn | Deep yellow | Clover | Ruby |

# Index

## Picture Acknowledgements

The Publishers would like to thank the following picture agencies for permission to reproduce their images in this book:

**Garden and Wildlife Matters:** 26l, 29, 38r, 45l, 47l, 48l, 50 both, 51l, 53 both, 55r, 56l, 60r.

**Images Colour Library:** 8 both, 10, 31br, 39r, 42r.

**Papilio Photographic:** 52r, 56r, 61r.

**Tony Stone Images:** 46r, 59r.

**Werner Foreman Archive:** 9, 28.

**York Archaeological Trust:** 51r.

Key: l = left, r = right, b = bottom.